AFTER HIGH SCHOOL

by Brian Harris, B.A., M. Ed.

A Guide To Help You
Plan Your Future After High School

ISBN 978-1460906293

Every effort has been made to ensure that the information
contained in this book is accurate. Neither the publisher
nor the author is engaged in rendering professional advice
or services to the individual reader. The ideas, strategies
and suggestions contained in this book are not intended
as a substitute for consulting with appropriate professionals.
Neither the author nor the publisher shall be liable or
responsible for any loss or damage allegedly arising
from any information or suggestions in this book.

CGS COMMUNICATIONS, INC.

TABLE OF CONTENTS

**If it is to be,
it is up to me!**

INTRODUCTION

Do you ever wonder what you are going to do after you finish high school? Do you sometimes wonder whether you should go to college or university, or take some other type of educational/training program after high school? And, if you decide to go to college or university, do you sometimes wonder what program you will take? Do you sometimes worry that you might take the wrong program and waste all the money it costs to attend college or university? If you answered YES to any of these questions, you are not alone. In research I have conducted with thousands of high school students, the number one cause of stress identified by many students was related to what they were going to do when they completed high school. In more than twenty years of helping high school students plan their future I have seen many students reduce this stress and be more successful by using the planning strategies provided in this book.

Rob was a grade 11 student who spent so much time worrying about what he was going to do after high school that he was barely passing his high school courses. He couldn't decide whether he wanted to go to college or do something else because he had no idea what he would study if he went. There were days when he wondered if he would even have the marks to get accepted to any kind of educational program after high school. With the completion of activities similar to those you will find in this book, Rob was able to identify his strengths. Once he understood that the best way to plan his future was to build on these strengths he was able to identify a program that best matched his interests, abilities and values. Remarkably, once he set a goal for his future, his marks in high school dramatically increased. By the end of grade 11, his course

Do you sometimes worry about what you are going to do when you finish high school?

Once you discover a focus for your future, you will experience greater success in all that you do.

marks had increased by almost 25%, and in grade 12 his course marks increased another 8%. Rob graduated from high school and entered a college program that he loved. After graduating from college, he found a job that provided great satisfaction for him (and once again matched his interests, abilities and values).

As you think about your future, one of the most important things for you to realize is that you have to take responsibility for yourself. Some people go through life thinking that the world owes them a job, or even owes them happiness. Unfortunately for these people, they will find discouragement and a lack of fulfillment throughout their lives. They will spend much of their time blaming others (including bosses, family, friends, and even the government) for their failures without realizing that they are their own problem. The person most responsible for the life you live is you.

Jasmine was a grade 12 student who experienced problems with her parents. Whenever she did poorly in school or whenever she had a fight with her friends, she would always shrug and say to herself, "Nothing ever goes right at home so why should I expect school to be any different?" A person like Jasmine could go through her entire life blaming others for her lack of success in whatever she does. In the end, Jasmine will always get exactly what she thinks she is going to get. If she sees herself as a failure, she will always be a failure. Eventually, we all become the kind of person that we see in our minds every day.

Success begins when you take 100% responsibility for your life. George Washington Carver said, "Ninety-nine percent of all failures come from people who have a habit of making excuses." When things aren't going the way you

You may not be able to change the world around you, but you can always change yourself.

The person most responsible for the life you live is you.

would like them to be going, the first person to look at is yourself. Even when negative things happen to you that you have no control over, you can decide how you will react to what has happened. A positive person will see obstacles and setbacks as temporary problems and will seek ways to overcome them.

AFTER HIGH SCHOOL gives you an opportunity to start to plan your future. As you begin to set some goals related to your interests, abilities and values, develop a picture in your mind of being successful in achieving these goals. Every day, visualize yourself achieving your goals. As you do this, you will find yourself beginning to complete what you need to do to be successful.

AFTER HIGH SCHOOL can assist you as you attempt to plan your future education/training. Your results will also help you to better understand which careers might be best for you. For most students the right career is not just one magical job. There are generally several occupations within a field that best match your interests, abilities and values. Later in this book you will see how your interests, abilities and values can correspond to groups of "related careers". Understanding the concept of related careers within career fields can not only help you find the best job after you graduate from your future education/training, but at some point if you find yourself unemployed (or underemployed), understanding this concept can help you to find your best occupation once again.

It is recommended that you take your time and think carefully as you complete this book. Don't attempt to complete the material in this book in one evening. After each chapter, take a day or two to think about what you have done. It is also recommended that you share your results

Eventually, you will become the kind of person you see yourself as being.

Throughout this book the words "job", "occupation" and "career" are used to mean the same thing.

Cherish your visions and your dreams as they are the blueprints of your ultimate achievements.

with your high school counselor/advisor and others who know you well, including your parents.

Chapter 1 gives you the opportunity to explore your interests as they relate to your experiences at high school. This chapter will also help you to form a beginning list of possible future career choices although you will explore the appropriateness of this list throughout the book. Whatever you love to do in high school (or as an interest when you are out of school) should be explored as a possibility for your future education/training. A basic theme throughout this book is that building on your strengths is one of the best approaches to achieving success in your life.

Chapter 2 explores your abilities. Most students will find that their interests and abilities go hand in hand, but if you become aware that the things that you are most interested in are different than what you do well, then this is an important area to resolve before you can successfully plan your future.

Chapter 3 will help you to identify your values and understand their importance in planning your future. Chapter 4 will help you to identify a future plan after high school based on your interests, abilities and values. And finally, Chapter 5 will help you to better understand how to achieve your goals.

Although the first few chapters of this book can help you to better understand how your future career choice is related to your interests, abilities and values, it is important to realize that many high school students will successfully plan their immediate future after high school without knowing the exact occupation they will some day pursue. There will be more thoughts on this throughout the book.

SUCCESS TIPS

1. Write a list of reasons how doing better
at school will help you.

2. Whenever you are successful,
repeat whatever you did again and again.

3. Thank others when they give you feedback
that will help you.

4. It is okay to adjust your goals.

5. Keep a picture in your mind of being successful.

6. Everyone faces problems.
The key to success is how you deal with them.

7. Learn from your failures and mistakes.

8. Take action, one small step at a time,
in the direction of your goals.

9. Build on your strengths.

10. Find someone else who has already
achieved what you want to do
and ask them for help.

Any form of work is far more enjoyable when you are doing something that you are interested in.

IDENTIFYING YOUR INTERESTS

For many years, Kelly planned to become a nurse after high school. She choose the high school courses she needed to enter a college program and worked very hard to obtain the required marks to ensure she would be admitted into the program. She held several part-time jobs to save some money to help pay for her future education. As Kelly left high school at the end of the school year, she was thrilled that she would soon be pursuing her dreams in nursing.

Ten months later I was walking through a local shopping mall and discovered Kelly selling clothes in a retail store. When I asked her how college was going, she said that she had dropped out. I immediately wondered how someone who seemed to be so set in her future plans could have experienced disappointment so quickly.

After a brief conversation with Kelly, I found out three things:

1) she strongly disliked some of the courses that were a part of her nursing program.
2) she realized her heart was not set on nursing as much as she thought it was, and that her determination for many years to become a nurse was really based on the dreams of others for her and not necessarily her own.
3) what she really loved to do was write, but she had never given this serious thought in planning her future.

Unfortunately, Kelly's story is not unusual. For some

The most successful people love what they do and do what they love.

students, once they find they have made a wrong decision in their future education/training, it is often then too expensive to begin again. Many of these students complete the program they are in (and then face a career they really don't want) or drop out of their educational or training program. How can you prevent this from happening to you?

The best answer to this question is to carefully consider what you love to do (and can do very well!) and then plan your future education/training based on these strengths.

In this first chapter of *AFTER HIGH SCHOOL*, you will begin to explore your interests. What are the things that you are most interested in? What do you like to talk about? What do you like to do? What things do you get excited about?

There is a tendency for all of us to move towards whatever we picture in our minds. We become what we think about the most, whether this is good for us or not. Unsuccessful people (and those who are miserable) often blame others for their failures, yet it is often this very picture of being unsuccessful that is locked into their minds that prevents them from becoming successful. Change your picture and you can change your life. This first chapter can help you to focus on your interests, and use this as a basis for thinking about your future in a manner that will help you to be more successful.

As you create a clearer picture in your mind as to what you love to do and what you do well (as explored in the next chapter), you can begin to create an image of your future. Create a positive image of being successful in whatever you decide to do and you will begin to move towards accomplishing your goals. The first step for this to become a reality is for you to identify your dream. The first three chapters of this book can help you to crystallize a vision for your future. They can also help you to better understand whether your dream is realistic for you.

You can create a blueprint for your life. In working with high school students, I often found students who were worried about their future because they had no idea what they wanted to do with their life. Perhaps you are like this and that is why you are reading this book. In this chapter as you explore your interests, you will be taking your first step towards successfully planning your future after high school. You will have the opportunity to identify your interests by choosing answers to a series of questions. It is important that you answer each question by selecting the response that is best for you. If you choose answers that are based on what you think others expect of you, you might find yourself like Kelly in a post-secondary program that becomes unbearable. Once you identify your interests, you will have taken the first step towards creating a plan for your future that will lead to a career that is satisfying for you.

There is no time limit on completing the questions in this chapter so sit back, take your time and carefully think about each of your responses. In PART A (pages 14 - 17), you will answer YES or NO to each of the statements given. You must choose YES or NO for each question. In PART B (pages 18 - 22), you will select two statements from each group of eight. It is important that you select two statements for each group.

Instructions will be provided on page 23 - 26 to help you understand how your interests relate to future planning.

"It's a funny thing about life; if you refuse to accept anything but the best, you very often get it."
W. Somerset Maugham

IDENTIFYING YOUR INTERESTS - PART A

> **INSTRUCTIONS:** Circle YES or NO for each of the following:

Do you enjoy, or do you think you would enjoy ...

1	researching important historical events	YES	NO	1
2	researching the effect of interest rates on stock market trends	YES	NO	2
3	sketching pictures	YES	NO	3
4	solving mathematical problems	YES	NO	4
5	helping to coach a sports team	YES	NO	5
6	learning about scientific theories	YES	NO	6
7	achieving a high level of proficiency on a musical instrument or voice	YES	NO	7
8	making a class presentation speaking in a language other than English	YES	NO	8
9	designing new computer software	YES	NO	9
10	writing a creative story	YES	NO	10
11	working as a volunteer to help others in your community	YES	NO	11
12	working with machinery or power tools	YES	NO	12
13	analyzing a dramatic performance	YES	NO	13
14	learning about ancient civilizations	YES	NO	14
15	starting your own business	YES	NO	15
16	experimenting with different techniques for painting a picture	YES	NO	16
17	graphing equations	YES	NO	17
18	learning about new advances in exercise techniques	YES	NO	18
19	completing experiments related to the laws of dynamics	YES	NO	19
20	performing on a musical instrument or voice before a large audience	YES	NO	20
21	translating newspaper articles from one language to another	YES	NO	21
22	administering a website	YES	NO	22
23	studying the content and style of great literary works	YES	NO	23
24	helping as a teaching assistant in one of your classes	YES	NO	24
25	using a software program to design a house	YES	NO	25
26	practicing improvisation and role playing	YES	NO	26
27	completing a project on urban planning	YES	NO	27
28	learning advertising techniques for marketing new products	YES	NO	28

Do you enjoy, or do you think you would enjoy . . .

29	researching a project on the life of a famous artist	YES	NO	29
30	employing exponential functions to model real world solutions	YES	NO	30
31	researching the mechanics of human body movements	YES	NO	31
32	completing a project on an ecosystem	YES	NO	32
33	studying musical theory	YES	NO	33
34	writing an essay using a language other than your first language	YES	NO	34
35	designing security features for an email system	YES	NO	35
36	writing articles for a magazine or newspaper	YES	NO	36
37	studying the psychology of human behavior	YES	NO	37
38	completing an electronics project	YES	NO	38
39	auditioning for a part in a local theatre presentation	YES	NO	39
40	researching different cultures	YES	NO	40
41	completing accounting assignments	YES	NO	41
42	analyzing the technical theory behind famous works of art	YES	NO	42
43	solving algebraic equations	YES	NO	43
44	completing a project related to nutrition	YES	NO	44
45	conducting chemistry experiments	YES	NO	45
46	practicing a musical instrument or voice for at least 1 hour every day .	YES	NO	46
47	reading a novel in a language other than your first language	YES	NO	47
48	using computer software to edit a video	YES	NO	48
49	discussing books you have read	YES	NO	49
50	tutoring a student who has learning problems	YES	NO	50
51	repairing an engine	YES	NO	51
52	researching a project on contemporary theatre	YES	NO	52
53	presenting a project on solutions to environmental problems	YES	NO	53
54	reading about the rights of employees in the workplace	YES	NO	54
55	sculpting a face using clay	YES	NO	55
56	solving problems related to financial applications	YES	NO	56
57	organizing and running a house league tournament	YES	NO	57
58	investigating the changes and relationships in chemical systems	YES	NO	58

Do you enjoy, or do you think you would enjoy . . .

59	composing music	YES	NO	59
60	learning the vocabulary of a language other than your first language .	YES	NO	60
61	designing a website for a business	YES	NO	61
62	studying the works of famous authors such as Shakespeare	YES	NO	62
63	working as a volunteer in a local hospital	YES	NO	63
64	assisting in building a house	YES	NO	64
65	creating and presenting a dramatic short play	YES	NO	65
66	exploring different political systems	YES	NO	66
67	completing a project on factors that affect our economy	YES	NO	67
68	drawing or painting copies of famous works of art	YES	NO	68
69	exploring applications of compound interest to financial investments .	YES	NO	69
70	studying the psychology of being a champion athlete	YES	NO	70
71	reading about advances in microbiology	YES	NO	71
72	researching the lives of famous composers	YES	NO	72
73	interpreting someone speaking a foreign language you have learned .	YES	NO	73
74	installing and configuring key computer components	YES	NO	74
75	developing a presentation using software such as PowerPoint	YES	NO	75
76	learning the components of being an effective listener	YES	NO	76
77	helping to build a broadcast studio	YES	NO	77
78	studying theories of acting from different historical periods	YES	NO	78
79	writing an essay on the causes of a major war	YES	NO	79
80	reading about people who have achieved great success in a business	YES	NO	80
81	completing a graphic design assignment using a computer	YES	NO	81
82	completing a project on logarithmic functions	YES	NO	82
83	working as an instructor in a fitness club	YES	NO	83
84	completing a project on the human immune system	YES	NO	84
85	providing music lessons to younger students	YES	NO	85
86	learning the grammatical rules of a foreign language	YES	NO	86
87	setting up e-commerce capabilities on a business website	YES	NO	87
88	making presentations to groups of people	YES	NO	88

Do you enjoy, or do you think you would enjoy . . .

89	assisting elderly people	YES	NO	89
90	completing a course in welding	YES	NO	90
91	writing an essay analyzing a work of dramatic literature	YES	NO	91
92	reading about solutions to help resolve world hunger	YES	NO	92
93	learning about e-commerce trends	YES	NO	93
94	experimenting with light and contrast in creating designs	YES	NO	94
95	solving problems involving vectors in 2 + 3 dimensional space	YES	NO	95
96	completing a project on living a healthy lifestyle	YES	NO	96
97	learning about molecular genetics	YES	NO	97
98	using a computer to arrange a musical selection	YES	NO	98
99	studying a series of short stories written in a second language for you	YES	NO	99
100	writing computer programs to drive devices such as robots	YES	NO	100
101	using a computer to compose letters and/ or organize reports	YES	NO	101
102	researching a project on the changing structure of families	YES	NO	102
103	installing mechanical devices	YES	NO	103
104	creating an original screenplay	YES	NO	104

Congratulations on finishing PART A.
Take a break before you begin PART B.
After you complete PART B,
you will be given further instructions
on how to interpret your results.

IDENTIFYING YOUR INTERESTS - PART B

INSTRUCTIONS: Select the two statements that you would enjoy doing the most from each group of eight. Write the corresponding numbers of these two statements in the boxes to the right of each group of eight.

1. researching important historical events
2. achieving a high level of proficiency on a musical instrument or voice
3. researching the effect of interest rates on stock market trends
4. solving mathematical problems
5. making a class presentation speaking in a language other than English
6. learning about scientific theories
7. helping to coach a sports team
8. sketching pictures

☐

☐

9. designing new computer software
10. writing a creative story
11. working as a volunteer to help others in your community
12. working with machinery or power tools
13. analyzing a dramatic performance
14. learning about ancient civilizations
15. experimenting with different techniques for painting a picture
16. starting your own business

☐

☐

17. performing on a musical instrument or voice before a large audience
18. completing experiments related to the laws of dynamics
19. learning about new advances in exercise techniques
20. helping as a teaching assistant in one of your classes
21. translating newspaper articles from one language to another
22. administering a website
23. studying the content and style of great literary works
24. graphing equations

☐

☐

INSTRUCTIONS: Select the two statements that you would enjoy doing the most from each group of eight. Write the corresponding numbers of these two statements in the boxes to the right of each group of eight.

25. using a software program to design a house
26. practicing improvisation and role playing
27. completing a project on urban planning
28. learning advertising techniques for marketing new products
29. researching a project on the life of a famous artist
30. employing exponential functions to model real world situations
31. researching the mechanics of human body movements
32. completing a project on an ecosystem

33. auditioning for a part in a local theatre presentation
34. writing an essay using a language other than your first language
35. designing security features for an email system
36. writing articles for a magazine or newspaper
37. studying the psychology of human behavior
38. completing an electronics project
39. studying musical theory
40. researching different cultures

41. completing accounting assignments
42. analyzing the technical theory behind famous works of art
43. conducting chemistry experiments
44. practicing a musical instrument or voice for at least one hour every day
45. completing a project related to nutrition
46. solving algebraic equations
47. reading a novel in a language other than your first language
48. using computer software to edit a video

49. discussing books you have read
50. tutoring a student who has learning problems
51. repairing an engine
52. researching a project on contemporary theatre
53. sculpting a face using clay
54. presenting a project on solutions to environmental problems
55. reading about the rights of employees in the workplace
56. solving problems related to financial applications

57. organizing and running a house league tournament
58. investigating the changes and relationships in chemical systems
59. learning the vocabulary of a language other than your first language
60. working as a volunteer in a local hospital
61. designing a website for a business
62. studying the works of famous authors such as Shakespeare
63. composing music
64. assisting in building a house

65. creating and presenting a dramatic short play
66. exploring different political systems
67. completing a project on factors that affect our economy
68. drawing or painting copies of famous works of art
69. exploring applications of compound interest to financial investments
70. researching the lives of famous composers
71. reading about advances in microbiology
72. studying the psychology of being a champion athlete

73. helping to build a broadcast studio
74. installing and configuring key computer components
75. developing a presentation using software such as PowerPoint
76. learning the components of being an effective listener
77. interpreting someone speaking a foreign language you have learned
78. studying theories of acting from different historical periods
79. completing a graphic design assignment using a computer
80. writing an essay on the causes of a major war

81. reading about people who have achieved great success in a business
82. completing a project on logarithmic functions
83. working as an instructor in a fitness club
84. completing a project on the human immune system
85. learning the grammatical rules of a foreign language
86. providing music lessons to younger students
87. setting up e-commerce capabilities on a business website
88. making presentations to groups of people

89. assisting elderly people
90. completing a course in welding
91. writing an essay analyzing a work of dramatic literature
92. solving problems involving vectors in 2 + 3 dimensional space
93. reading about solutions to help resolve world hunger
94. experimenting with light and contrast in creating designs
95. learning about e-commerce trends
96. completing a project on living a healthy lifestyle

97. learning about molecular genetics
98. using a computer to arrange a musical selection
99. studying a series of short stories written in a second language for you
100. writing computer programs to drive devices such as robots
101. using a computer to compose and/or organize reports
102. researching a project on the changing structure of families
103. installing mechanical devices
104. creating an original screenplay

Congratulations on finishing PART B.
The next four pages will give you instructions
on how to interpret your results.
On these pages you will begin to see
how your interests relate to possible career choices.

"Where your interests meet the needs
of this world, there lies your vocation."
Aristotle

A SUMMARY OF YOUR INTERESTS - PART A

INSTRUCTIONS: On this page circle all the numbers that match your "YES" answers from pages 14 - 17. After you have circled the appropriate numbers, add the number of circles in each subject row and place this total at the end of the row under the heading "TOTALS".

SUBJECT AREA	QUESTION NUMBERS FROM PAGES 14 - 17								TOTALS
SOCIAL SCIENCE	1	14	27	40	53	66	79	92	
BUSINESS	2	15	28	41	54	67	80	93	
ART	3	16	29	42	55	68	81	94	
MATH-EMATICS	4	17	30	43	56	69	82	95	
RECREATION	5	18	31	44	57	70	83	96	
SCIENCE	6	19	32	45	58	71	84	97	
MUSIC	7	20	33	46	59	72	85	98	
LANGUAGES	8	21	34	47	60	73	86	99	
COMPUTERS	9	22	35	48	61	74	87	100	
ENGLISH	10	23	36	49	62	75	88	101	
SERVICE	11	24	37	50	63	76	89	102	
TECHNICAL	12	25	38	51	64	77	90	103	
DRAMATIC ARTS	13	26	39	52	65	78	91	104	

A SUMMARY OF YOUR INTERESTS - PART B

INSTRUCTIONS: On this page circle all the numbers that match your answers from pages 18 - 22. After you have circled the appropriate numbers, add the number of circles in each subject row and place this total at the end of the row under the heading "TOTALS". Note that the numbers are not necessarily in order.

SUBJECT AREA	QUESTION NUMBERS FROM PAGES 18 - 22								TOTALS
SOCIAL SCIENCE	1	14	27	40	54	66	80	93	
BUSINESS	3	16	28	41	55	67	81	95	
ART	8	15	29	42	53	68	79	94	
MATH-EMATICS	4	24	30	46	56	69	82	92	
RECREATION	7	19	31	45	57	72	83	96	
SCIENCE	6	18	32	43	58	71	84	97	
MUSIC	2	17	39	44	63	70	86	98	
LANGUAGES	5	21	34	47	59	77	85	99	
COMPUTERS	9	22	35	48	61	74	87	100	
ENGLISH	10	23	36	49	62	75	88	101	
SERVICE	11	20	37	50	60	76	89	102	
TECHNICAL	12	25	38	51	64	73	90	103	
DRAMATIC ARTS	13	26	33	52	65	78	91	104	

SUMMARIZING YOUR INTERESTS

INSTRUCTIONS: On the following chart place your total scores from page 23 in Column A and your scores from page 24 in Column B. In Column C add your scores for each interest area from Columns A and B.

INTEREST AREA	COLUMN A (from page 23)	COLUMN B (from page 24)	COLUMN C (from A + B)
SOCIAL SCIENCE			
BUSINESS			
ART			
MATHEMATICS			
RECREATION			
SCIENCE			
MUSIC			
LANGUAGES			
COMPUTERS			
ENGLISH			
SERVICE			
TECHNICAL			
DRAMATIC ARTS			

YOUR TOP THREE INTERESTS

On the above chart you can see the areas that you appear to have the strongest interest in by looking at your scores in Column C (NOTE: these are not necessarily the things that you do best. You will identify the things that you do best in the next chapter of this book).

On the chart below list your top three interest areas from the above chart (an extra space is provided in the event you have any ties).

INTEREST AREA	SCORE

A FIRST LOOK AT POSSIBLE CAREER CHOICES

INSTRUCTIONS: List your three highest interest areas from the bottom of page 25 with your highest interest area going in box 1 below; your second highest interest area in box 2 below; and your third highest interest area in box 3 below.

From the careers listed on pages 27 - 31, select 3 - 5 careers you think would be future possibilities for you from each of your highest three interest categories and write these careers in the appropriate boxes below. A sample box is provided to illustrate what you are to do.

SAMPLE BOX

If your highest interest score (from page 25) was in "BUSINESS", you would go to the BUSINESS list of careers on page 27 and then select 3 - 5 careers that are future possibilities for you from this list and enter them in this box. So for example, your list might look like this:

entrepreneur, financial planner, investment analyst

YOUR HIGHEST INTEREST AREA =

BOX 1

YOUR SECOND HIGHEST INTEREST AREA =

BOX 2

YOUR THIRD HIGHEST INTEREST AREA =

BOX 3

SOCIAL SCIENCE

ANTHROPOLOGIST
ARCHAEOLOGIST
ARCHIVIST
CHILD + YOUTH WORKER
COMMUNITY LEADER
CONSERVATION OFFICER
COUNSELOR
CURATOR
FAMILY SERVICES WORKER
FISHERIES OFFICER
FLIGHT ATTENDANT
FORESTRY PROFESSIONALS
GEOGRAPHER

GEOLOGICAL TECHNICIAN
GOVERNMENT OFFICER
HISTORIAN
HOTEL WORKERS
HUMAN RESOURCES MANAGER
HUMAN RIGHTS OFFICER
IMMIGRATION OFFICER
INFORMATION ANALYST
JOURNALIST
LABOR RELATIONS OFFICER
LAND SURVEYOR
LAND USE PLANNER
LAWYER

LIBRARIAN
MARKET RESEARCHER
MINING SUPERVISOR
MUSEUM EDUCATORS
NEWS ANALYST
PARALEGAL
POLITICAL ORGANIZER
PSYCHOLOGIST
REAL ESTATE SALES-
PERSON
SOCIAL WORKER
TEACHER
TOURISM WORKER

BUSINESS

ACCOUNT EXECUTIVE
ACCOUNTANT
ACCOUNTS PAYABLE CLERK
ACTUARY
ADMINISTRATIVE ASSISTANT
ADMINISTRATIVE MANAGER
ANALYST
APPRAISER
AUDITOR
BANK WORKER
BUDGET SUPERVISOR
BUYER
CASHIER

CHIEF EXECUTIVE OFFICER
CLAIMS ADJUSTER
COST ESTIMATOR
CUSTOMER SERVICES
CUSTOMS BROKER
DATA ENTRY CLERK
ECONOMIST
EMPLOYEE RELATIONS
ENTREPRENEUR
EXECUTIVE ASSISTANT
FINANCIAL PLANNER
HUMAN RESOURCES MANAGER
INVESTMENT ANALYST

LAWYER
LEASING SERVICES
LOAN OFFICER
MARKETING ANALYST
OFFICE ASSISTANT
PARALEGAL
RECEPTIONIST
RETAIL PERSONNEL
SALESPERSON
SECRETARY
TELEMARKETER
WEB SPECIALIST

ART

ADVERTISING DESIGNER
ANIMATOR
ANTIQUE DEALER
ARCHITECT
ARCHITECTURAL TECHNI-
CIAN
ART DEALER
ARTIST
ARTISTIC DIRECTOR
BAKER
CABINETMAKER
CAD TECHNOLOGIST
CLOTHING DESIGNER

COSMETICIAN
CRAFTSPERSON
CURATOR
DECORATOR
DESIGN TECHNICIAN
DISPLAY DESIGNER
ESTHETICIAN
FASHION DESIGNER
FILM EDITOR
FLORIST
FURNITURE DESIGNER
GAMES DESIGNER
GRAPHIC ARTIST

HAIRSTYLIST
ILLUSTRATOR
INTERIOR DESIGNER
LANDSCAPE ARCHITECT
PHOTO EDITOR
POTTER
SCULPTOR
SET DESIGNER
TEACHER/INSTRUCTOR
WARDROBE SUPERVISOR
WEBSITE ARTIST
WEBSITE DESIGNER

MATHEMATICS

ACCOUNTANT	CONTRACTOR	PAYROLL OFFICER
ACCOUNTNG CLERK	COST ESTIMATOR	PHARMACIST
ACTUARY	CREDIT MANAGER	PILOT
AGRICULTURAL PROFESSIONAL	ENGINEER	PRODUCT DESIGNER
ANALYST	ENGINEERING TECHNICIAN	PURCHASING AGENT
ARCHITECT	FINANCIAL PLANNER	SALES REPRESENTATIVES
AUDITOR	INCOME TAX SPECIALIST	SCIENCE PROFESSIONAL
BANKING CLERK	INSURANCE BROKER	SECURITIES TRADER
CASHIER	INVESTMENT ANALYST	STATISTICIAN
CHEF	LASER TECHNICIAN	SYSTEMS CONTROLS
CHEMIST	LOANS OFFICER	TEACHER/INSTRUCTOR
COMPUTER PROGRAMMER	MARKET ANALYST	WEB ARCHITECT
COMPUTER TECHNICIAN	MECHANIC	

RECREATION

ATHLETE	FLIGHT ATTENDANT	RESORT STAFF
ATHLETIC THERAPIST	FOOD SERVICES WORKER	RESTAURANT STAFF
BANQUET STAFF	GUEST + HOTEL SERVICES	RETIREMENT COUNSELOR
CHEF	LANDSCAPE WORKER	RETIREMENT SERVICES
CONVENTION WORKER	KINESIOLOGIST	SALES PERSONNEL
CORPORATE TRAVEL	LEISURE CONSULTANT	TICKET AGENT
DANCE THERAPIST	LIFESTYLE PLANNER	TOUR GUIDE
DANCER	PARKS MANAGER	TOUR OPERATOR
ENTERTAINER	PARKS WORKER	TOURISM COORDINATOR
EVENT MANAGEMENT	PHYSIOTHERAPIST	TRAVEL AGENT
EVENT STAFF	PHYSIOTHERAPIST AIDE	TRAVEL WRITER
FITNESS CONSULTANT	RECREATION DIRECTOR	WAITER/WAITRESS
FITNESS INSTRUCTOR	RECREATION PLANNER	

SCIENCE

AGRICULTURAL EXPERT	DENTAL TECHNICIAN	LABORATORY TESTER
ANIMAL CARE TECHNICIAN	DENTIST	LANDSCAPE ARCHITECT
ANIMAL HEALTH TECHNOLO-	DIETICIAN	MEDICAL ASSISTANT
GIST	DOCTOR	MEDICAL SECRETARY
AUDIOLOGIST	ENGINEER	NURSE
BIOCHEMIST	FISHERIES PROFESSIONAL	NURSING ASSISTANT
BIOLOGIST	FORENSIC CHEMIST	OPTOMETRIST
BIOMEDICAL TECHNICIAN	FORESTRY PROFESSIONAL	PHARMACIST
CHEMIST	GENETICIST	RESPIRATORY TECHNICIAN
CHIROPRACTOR	GREENHOUSE MANAGER	VETERINARIAN
CHIROPRACTOR AIDE	HEALTH CARE AIDE	VETERINARIAN ASSISTANT
CLINICAL LEADER	HORTICULTURIST	X-RAY TECHNICIAN
CONSERVATION OFFFICER	LAB TECHNOLOGIST	

MUSIC

ACTOR	MULTIMEDIA SOUND TECH.	PROFESSIONAL MUSICIAN
ANNOUNCER/BROADCASTER	MUSIC ARRANGER	PUBLICIST
CHOREOGRAPHER	MUSIC COORDINATOR	RECORDING PRODUCER
COMPOSER	MUSIC COPYIST	RECORDING TECHNICIAN
CONDUCTOR	MUSIC CRITIC	SINGER
DANCER	MUSIC LIBRARIAN	SOUND EDITOR
ENTERTAINER	MUSIC SALESPERSON	STAGE BAND MEMBER
ENTERTAINMENT ORGANIZER	MUSIC THERAPIST	STAGE CREW
EVENT STAFF	MUSIC VIDEO DIRECTOR	STUDIO MANAGER
INSTRUCTOR/TEACHER	MUSICAL INSTRUMENT TUNER	TALENT SCOUT
INSTRUMENT REPAIRER	MUSICAL THEATRE DIRECTOR	VIDEOGRAPHER
INSTRUMENT SALESPERSON	MUSICAL THEATRE STAFF	VIDEO DIRECTOR
MULTIMEDIA PRODUCER	PERFORMING ARTIST	

LANGUAGES

ANNOUNCER/BROADCASTER	GOVERNMENT WORKER	PUBLIC RELATIONS WORK-
BUYER	HOTEL MANAGER	ER
CAREGIVER	HOTEL SERVICES WORKER	RECEPTIONIST
CASHIER	HUMAN RIGHTS OFFICER	RESORT STAFF
CHAUFFEUR	IMMIGRATION OFFICER	RESTAURANT STAFF
CHIEF EXECUTIVE OFFICER	INTERNATIONAL RELATIONS	SALESPERSON
COMMUNITY WORKER	INTERPRETER	SPEECH PATHOLOGIST
CUSTOMER RELATIONS	JOURNALIST	TAXI DRIVER
CUSTOMER SERVICES	LAWYER	TOUR GUIDE
EMPLOYEE RELATONS	LIBRARIAN	TRANSLATOR
FAMILY SERVICES WORKER	LINGUIST	TRAVEL AGENT
FLIGHT ATTENDANT	NEWS ANALYST	TRAVEL + TOURISM
FLIGHT SERVICES	POLITICAL ORGANIZER	WAITER/WAITRESS

COMPUTERS

APPLICATIONS ENGINEER	ENGINEER	PROTOCOL SPECIALIST
APPLICATIONS SUPPORT	FIREWALL TEST ENGINEER	SALES REPRESENTATIVE
BUSINESS INFO. ANALYST	GRAPHICS DESIGNER	SECURITY SPECIALIST
BUSINESS SYSTEMS SPE-	HARDWARE DESIGNER	SOFTWARE DEVELOPER
CIALIST	HARDWARE INSTALLER	SOLUTION ARCHITECT
COMPUTER ANALYST	HELP DESK SUPPORT	SYSTEMS ANALYST
COMPUTER PROGRAMMER	INSTALLATION SERVICES	TECHNICAL WRITER
COMPUTER TECHNICIAN	INTERNET SOLUTIONS TECH.	TEACHER/INSTRUCTOR
CONFIGURATION MANAGER	MARKET RESEARCHER	TESTER
CUSTOMER ENGINEER	MASTER SCHEDULER	VIDEO/FILM EDITOR
DATA ARCHITECT	MULTIMEDIA INTERFACE	WEBSITE ADMINISTRATOR
DATABASE ADMINISTRATOR	NETWORK ADMINISTRATOR	WEBSITE DESIGNER
E-BUSINESS CONSULTANT	PRODUCT DEVELOPER	

ENGLISH

ACTOR	FILM CRITIC	MARKETING DIRECTOR
ADMINISTRATOR	FILM DIRECTOR	NEWS EDITOR
ADVERTISING DIRECTOR	HISTORIAN	NOVELIST
ANNOUNCER/BROADCASTER	HUMAN RESOURCES MANAGER	PARALEGAL
ARCHIVIST	INSURANCE BROKER	PROOFREADER
AUTHOR	JOURNALIST	PUBLICIST
BOOK CRITIC	LAWYER	RECEPTIONIST
COMMUNICATIONS EXPERT	LEGISLATOR	SALESPERSON
CUSTOMER SERVICES	LIBRARIAN	SECRETARY
DATA ENTRY CLERK	LIBRARY ASSISTANT	SPEECH PATHOLOGIST
DISPATCHER	LINGUIST	TELEMARKETER
EDITOR	MANAGER	WRITER
EDITORIAL ASSISTANT	MARKETING ANALYST	

SERVICE

AMBULANCE ATTENDANT	GERIATRIC WORKER	PARAMEDIC
BEREAVEMENT CONSELOR	HAIRSTYLIST	PERSONAL SUPPORT
CAREER ADVISOR	HOME HEALTH AIDE	WORKER
CASHIER	HOTEL SERVICES	PERSONNEL MANAGER
CHILD + YOUTH WORKER	HUMAN RESOURCES MANAGER	PHYSICIAN
CORRECTIONAL OFFICER	LABOR RELATIONS SPECIALIST	PHYSIOTHERAPIST
COUNSELOR	LAWYER	POLICE OFFICER
CUSTOMER SERVICES	LEGAL ASSISTANT	PSYCHIATRIST
DAY CARE WORKER	MASSAGE THERAPIST	RECREATON LEADER
DENTAL ASSISTANT	NANNY	REHABILITATION SERVICES
FIREFIGHTER	NURSE	SOCIAL WORKER
FLIGHT SERVICES	OCCUPATIONAL THERAPIST	SPECIAL NEEDS WORKER
FUNERAL SERVICES	PARALEGAL	TEACHER

TECHNICAL

APPLIANCE SERVICE	CEMENT MASON	HEAVY EQUIPMENT OPER-
ARCHITECT	CLEANING SERVICES	ATOR
ARCHITECTURAL TECH.	COMPUTER REPAIRS	INDUSTRIAL DESIGNER
ASSEMBLER	CONTRACTOR	LANDSCAPE ARCHITECT
BACKHOE OPERATOR	CONSTRUCTION MANAGER	MACHINE DESIGNER
BOILERMAKER	DRILLER	MECHANIC
BRICKLAYER	DRIVERS, BUS + TRUCK	MILLWRIGHT
BUTCHER	ELECTRICIAN	MINING WORKER
CABINETMAKER	ENGINEER	PLUMBER
CABLE INSTALLER	ENGINEERING TECHNICIAN	PRODUCT DESIGNER
CAD TECHNOLOGIST	FIREFIGHTER	ROOFER
CARPENTER	FISHERMAN/WOMAN	SERVICE TECHNICIAN
CARPET CLEANER	FORKLIFT OPERATOR	WELDER

DRAMATIC ARTS

ACTOR
ANNOUNCER/BROADCASTER
CAMERA OPERATOR
CHOREOGRAPHER
CLOWN
COLUMNIST
COMMUNICATIONS EXPERT
DANCE THERAPIST
DANCER
DIRECTOR
DRAMA COACH
FACILITIES MANAGER
FILMMAKER

MAGICIAN
MAKE-UP ARTIST
MAKE-UP CONSULTANT
MODEL
MUSEUM GUIDE
MUSICIAN
PERFORMER
PRODUCER
PROFESSIONAL SPEAKER
PUBLICIST
PUPPETEER
RECORDING TECHNICIAN
SALESPERSON

SCRIPT SUPERVISOR
SCRIPT WRITER
SET DESIGNER
SINGER
SPEECH WRITER
STAGE DIRECTOR
TALENT SCOUT
TEACHER/INSTRUCTOR
THEATRE STAFF
WAITER/WAITRESS
WARDROBE SUPERVISOR
WRITER

ADDITIONAL CAREERS

INSTRUCTIONS: In this box write any occupations that you are interested in that are not already listed on pages 27 - 31.

BOX 4

**Your greatest success
will come from focusing
on what you do best.**

IDENTIFYING YOUR ABILITIES

You are now ready to identify your abilities. In Chapter 1 you identified your interests. Interests are the things you enjoy doing, but they are not necessarily the things you do the best.

At the age of eighteen Jeff dreamed of being a professional baseball player. If anyone asked him what he loved to do, he would say he loved to play baseball. Baseball was his strong interest. Unfortunately for Jeff, baseball was not the thing he did best. Jeff had poor coordination, was a slow runner, threw a baseball poorly, and rarely hit the ball. In other words, the thing that Jeff enjoyed doing the most was not the thing he was best at. His abilities did not match his interests. Even after hours of practice and years of trying, his abilities were not improving. What Jeff loved to do was play baseball, but what he did really well (with very little effort) was running a small business he had developed.

Identifying and understanding the things that you can do very well is another part of planning your future. You may find that what you do well is exactly the same as what you are interested in. On the other hand, you might discover that what you do well is not the same as the things you are most interested in. Later in this book you will learn how to combine your interests and abilities (whether they are the same or not) to plan your future.

Successful people focus on what they do best. When you are able to identify and understand the things that you

**Successful people
focus
on
what they do
best.**

love to do and do well, you will have taken a big step forward towards your future success. When your future education/training is based on pursuing your strengths, you will find your future education/training exciting. You will look forward to your classes each day because you are doing what you really want to do.

When you spend most of your time and energy doing what you do best and love to do, it will be easier for you to achieve success. To discover your abilities, ask yourself a few questions. What is something you can do better than most other people? What is something you do that doesn't seem like work for you? What is something that you do that others compliment you on? Throughout this chapter you will be exploring answers to these questions.

Below, and on the next few pages, is a list of ability categories and a brief description of the school courses and interests that are associated with each one. The ability categories are given in alphabetical order. It is important to realize that the school subjects listed under each category may not all be offered at your high school. In some cases there may be subjects that you have studied that are not listed (if there is a school subject that you are strongly interested in, ask your parents or teachers which interest area that subject would best fit, and then add it to the appropriate category in this list). You will notice that some school subjects may be listed under more than one ability category. As you read the description of each ability category, begin to think about which category best describes your abilities.

ART: this includes courses and interests such as art, visual arts, graphic design, photography, printmaking, set design, retail design, drawing, sketching, illustration, painting, sculpting, pottery making, architecture and interior design.

"I have learned that if one advances confidently in the direction of his dreams, and endeavors to live the life he has imagined, he will meet with a success unexpected in common hours."
Henry David Thoreau

BUSINESS: this includes courses and interests such as business studies, communication studies, group dynamics, workplace ethics, financial management, investment strategies, accounting, entrepreneurship studies, marketing, economics, management theory, management fundamentals, information technology, e-business, and business law.

COMPUTERS: this includes courses and interests such as computers + information science, computer engineering, programming, software development, website development, website administration, designing computer components, e-business, constructing systems that use computer programs to interact with hardware and diagnosing hardware and software problems.

DRAMATIC ARTS: this includes courses and interests such as the exploration of dramatic forms and techniques, performing and analyzing drama, improvisation, role playing, acting, producing dramatic works, interpreting dramatic literature, directing theatrical productions and media studies.

ENGLISH: this includes courses and interests such as English studies, language arts, creative writing, persuasive writing, communication studies, analytical reading, communication skills, media studies, study of poetry, study of short stories, journalism, study of the works of famous authors and writing literary essays.

LANGUAGES: this includes courses and interests such as the study of a language other than your first language (defined here as a foreign language), oral communication of a foreign language, reading and writing a foreign language, study of customs associated with a foreign language, translating any form of communication from one language to another and studying literary + media works in a foreign language.

MATHEMATICS: this includes courses and interests such as mathematics, mathematical theories and related problem solving, algebra, geometry, trigonometry, graphing, accounting, functions, calculus and information management.

MUSIC: this includes courses and interests such as piano, voice, musical instrumentation, music theory, study of famous composers, arranging musical works, performing, analyzing music, recording + production techniques, study of music styles throughout various historical periods, practicing technical exercises and repertoire pieces,

> "Formulate and stamp indelibly on your mind a mental picture of yourself as succeeding."
> Norman Vincent Peale

composing, studying software related to creating music, and conducting techniques.

RECREATION: this includes courses and interests such as healthy active living, physical education, exercise techniques, sports, fitness, health, lifestyle choices, athletic competitions, organizing tournaments, movement principles, kinesiology, sports administration and recreation.

SCIENCE: this includes courses and interests such as scientific inquiry, biology, chemistry, physics, scientific theories, environment, ecosystems, scientific experimentation, genetics and scientific research.

SERVICE: this includes courses and interests such as volunteer work in the community or school, helping others, psychology, sociology, parenting, social work, medical studies, injury management, health care, teaching and counseling.

SOCIAL SCIENCE: this includes courses and interests such as history, geography, politics, humanities, parenting, world religions, family studies, environment, psychology, sociology, anthropology and archaeology.

TECHNICAL: this includes courses and interests such as engine repair/maintenance, vehicle repair/maintenance, working with machinery or power tools, carpentry, electrical, woodworking, construction, architecture, plumbing, instrumentation design, structural analysis and installation services.

OTHER: (list any other subject areas here that you have studied that were not already listed on pages 34 - 36)

"I know for sure that what we dwell on is who we become."
Oprah Winfrey

IDENTIFYING YOUR TOP ABILITIES

INSTRUCTIONS: On the chart below, list your top five high school ability categories from pages 34 - 36 (including any subjects that you added to this list) in order of strength for you.

For example, the number one ability category that you write below will be the area that describes the things you are best at doing. The second ability category that you write will be your next best area and so on.

If you are having difficulty with this task it might be useful for you to talk to a teacher or counselor. In addition, your past and present report card marks may provide some indication of your ability in each subject areas.

ART

BUSINESS

COMPUTERS

DRAMATIC ARTS

ENGLISH

LANGUAGES

MATHEMATICS

MUSIC

RECREATION

SCIENCE

SERVICE

SOCIAL SCIENCES

TECHNICAL

OTHER

PRIORITIZING MY ABILITY CATEGORIES

My top
five
abilities

1. . . . .

2. . . . .

3. . . . .

4. . . . .

5. . . . .

BOX 5

ANOTHER LOOK AT MY FUTURE PLANS

INSTRUCTIONS: In BOX #6 below, write the five careers from BOXES 1, 2 + 3 on page 26 and any other occupations from BOX #4 at the bottom of page 31 that you are most interested in.

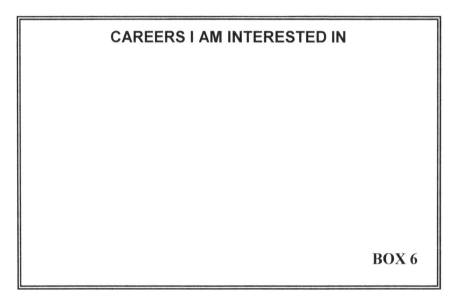

CAREERS I AM INTERESTED IN

BOX 6

INSTRUCTIONS: The occupations that you listed above (in BOX #6) were chosen by you based on your interests. On page 37 you identified your top subject areas at school. Circle any (or even all) careers in BOX #6 above that have the strongest relationship to your best five subjects in school (from BOX 5).

In other words, circle any careers in BOX 6 above that depend on you doing well in one or more of your top five subject areas from BOX 5 on page 37. If you are having any difficulties completing this, ask your teacher/counselor/parents for help.

MY TOP 3 CAREER CHOICES

INSTRUCTIONS: On page 38, you identified a list of your top careers (based on your interests). Next, you circled any occupations in this list that best matched your subject strengths at school. The careers that you circled would appear to be the ones that best match your abilities and interests.

In BOX 7 below, list the top 3 careers that would seem to best match your interests and abilities (and these will come from BOX 6 on page 38)

MY TOP 3 CAREER CHOICES
(based on my interests and abilities)

BOX 7

To help you better understand what is required to be successful to someday get hired into one of your top three career choices, next you should answer the questions on page 40. You can find the answers to these questions through research on the internet or by using resources in your school library or guidance department.

MY TOP CAREER CHOICE

1. From BOX #7 on page 39, I think that my top career choice at this time would be .
.

2. After high school, 2 - 3 colleges/universities or other training/educational institutions I could attend to help me get the qualifications for this career are . . .

3. The name of the college/university program (or a program from some other educational/training institution) that I would have to complete in order to become qualified for this career is . . .

4. In order to get accepted into the above program, in high school I would have to complete the following courses . . .

5. In addition to successfully completing the courses I identified in #4 above, I will also have to do the following to get accepted into the program that will help me get qualified for the career I would like to pursue. . .

RELATED CAREERS

INSTRUCTIONS: It is possible that you might plan for a future career, but unforeseen circumstances (such as a changing job market or not being accepted into the college/ university program that you want to enter) might prevent you from successfully achieving this career. When this happens it is beneficial to be aware that there are often many careers that are related to your main career choice. You might go in a slightly different direction while still choosing an occupation based on your interests and abilities. On the following chart, write your number one career choice (from page 40) in the circle in the middle of the chart. Next, write down all the careers that you can think of that are related. For example, if you wrote "doctor" in the middle circle some "related careers" might be nurse, medical supplies salesperson, x-ray technician, medical researcher, and so on.

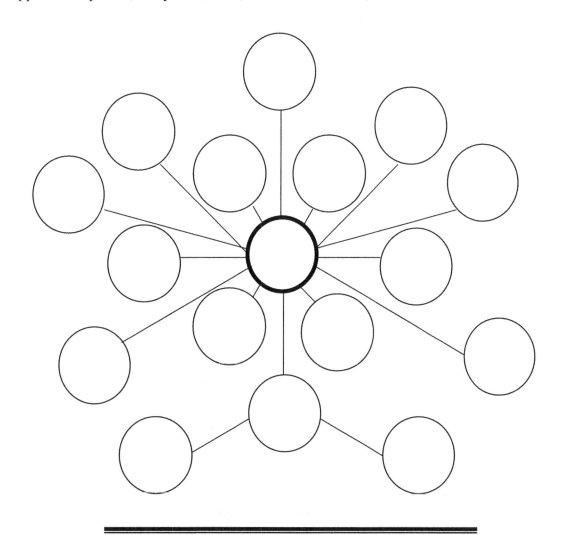

MORE TIPS ON ACHIEVING SUCCESS

1. Success is sometimes going from failure to failure without losing enthusiasm for what you really want to achieve.

2. There is no such thing as failure. Everything that you do is a lesson helping you to learn how to be more successful achieving your goals.

3. If you want to change your life, begin with changing yourself.

4. Excuses and blame are obstacles that can get in the way of being successful. The critical factor in becoming successful is to take 100% responsibility for your life.

5. The fastest way to achieve success is to find someone who is already successful in what you want to accomplish and then model what they do. If possible, ask this person if he/she can be a mentor for you.

6. Winners have developed certain habits. When your life is based on these same habits, you too will become a winner.

7. Keep a constant focus on what you want as though you have already achieved it.

8. Surround yourself with successful people.

9. You will achieve your greatest success when what you do every day is aligned with your interests, your abilities and your values.

10. No one achieves their dreams without a goal real enough to taste, a reason strong enough to move mountains, a strategy as specific as a roadmap, and a willingness to take action no matter what the circumstances.

A REVIEW OF WHAT YOU HAVE LEARNED SO FAR

At the beginning of this book it was stressed that most successful people build on their strengths. As a result, one of the best approaches to planning your future after high school is to begin by identifying your strengths and then identify career/educational/training possibilities that best match these strengths.

In the first chapter of this book you identified your interests by completing an interest survey. Once you had identified your interests, you were able to select some careers that best matched these.

In the second chapter, you explored your abilities. One way to identify some of your abilities is to consider which subjects in school you are best at doing. While this approach has the problem of not necessarily considering all your possible abilities, it can at least you give you an indication of some of the things you do well (especially as they relate to school success). It was also noted in this chapter that it makes sense to choose a future plan after high school based on both your interests and abilities. In this chapter, you had the opportunity to explore some of the requirements you would need to have to pursue specific educational/ training programs that might be available to you after high school. Finally, this chapter introduced the concept of related careers.

From my extensive experience in counseling high school students, I found that about 2/3 of students did not know what future career they wanted to pursue. If you are in that situation, an approach that you might want to consider is choosing a educational/training program after high school that best matches your interests and abilities. This way you are still building on your strengths, and at some later time (after high school) you will begin to better understand some of the careers that could result from your further education/training.

Your values are your personal success compass.

IDENTIFYING YOUR VALUES

Why Are Values Important To Consider In Planning Your Future?

To a very large degree your values will determine your satisfaction with whatever educational or training program you pursue after high school. What you value helps to create meaning in your life. For you to live your life to the fullest, it is important that your goals reflect your values. Your values are like a compass giving you direction. When your future planning follows the direction of your internal compass, as represented by your values, you will be enthusiastic and positive about whatever you are doing.

Mike graduated from high school with a desire to make a lot of money. He trained as a real estate agent. With strong communication skills and a passion to be successful, Mike was soon making the kind of money he had dreamed about. He bought an expensive condo, a great car, the best clothing and always had the money to do whatever he wanted. Unfortunately, though, Mike was not happy. Being a very successful real estate agent was not satisfying for him.

As Mike began to explore what was happening in his life, he thought about his past. In high school, Mike often volunteered with local community agencies to help kids who were experiencing problems. He always found great satisfaction in doing this. Helping others, especially children, was a core value for Mike. Although he hadn't recognized it at the time, this value was stronger for him than his

CHAPTER

3

"Personal leadership is the process of keeping your vision and values before you and aligning your life to be congruent with them"
Stephen Covey

desire to make a great deal of money. By ignoring this value, he had become unhappy even though he was very successful in his job.

Mike realized he could begin to do some volunteer work again, or use some of his money to help others, or he could even change careers. In Mike's situation, he gave up his lucrative career in real estate and went back to college to complete training to become a youth counselor.

After a few years of college, Mike began a new career in working with children. Although he would not likely earn as much money as he would have if he had remained in real estate, he found he was much happier working with kids.

What then is a value? A dictionary would define a value as:

- something of importance
- what something is worth
- the usefulness of something
- something you hold dear to you
- something you cherish
- something you regard highly and respect

A thesaurus would use some of the following words to describe value:

- worth, benefit, advantage
- importance, merit, significance
- usefulness, worthiness

As you begin to think of your values, ask yourself the following questions:

1) What is really important to you?
2) What is something you cherish about yourself?
3) What do you feel passionate about?

> **"Most people have the wrong idea of what constitutes true happiness. It is not attained through self-gratification but through devotion to a worthy purpose."**
> Helen Keller

As you go through life, all the decisions that you make will be impacted by your values. When you make decisions that align with your values, you will feel satisfied even if you face obstacles in what you are doing. If you make decisions that do not align with your values you may find yourself unhappy even though like Mike on the previous page you have achieved your initial goals.

When you know what is most important to you, your decisions become easier. You will find it easier to plan your future after high school when you are able to identify your core values. The following provides a list of some possible values (and a brief description of each value). These values are given in the context of what you would be looking for in a future career. Read the list and begin to think about which of these values is most important to you.

Taking your first step in the right direction is more important than taking many steps going the wrong way.

ADVANCEMENT: you would like the opportunity to rise or be promoted to increasing levels of expertise, management or leadership within a company or organization.

CHALLENGE: you would like a future career that offers challenges for you each day. This is a job where you will need to constantly keep learning in order to be able to handle new projects that you are involved in each day.

COMPETITIVE: you would like a career where you are competing against others as part of your job. You enjoy the prospect of constantly trying to be the best in comparison to others.

CREATIVE EXPRESSION: you would like a career that offers an opportunity for you to be very creative. This would tend to be a job where you could best employ your artistic talents or be inventive.

Most people struggle with success because of a lack of focus.

ENTREPRENEURIAL: you would like a career that offers you the opportunity to do things your way (preferably to start your own business). You tend to enjoy taking risks and you are very good at promoting what you do.

FOLLOWER: you would like a career where someone tells you each day exactly what you have to do and how to do it. Your job would be to primarily follow instructions rather than create new ways of doing things.

HELP OTHERS: you would like a career where you are given the opportunity to make a difference in the lives of others.

HIGH EARNINGS: you would like a career where you have the opportunity to make a lot of money.

INDEPENDENCE: you would like a career where you have the freedom to choose when and how you want to work. This job would give you the flexibility to choose what you want to do each day.

KNOWLEDGE: you would like a career where you are constantly learning. Your job allows you to work in research and the development of new ideas and possibilities.

LEADERSHIP: you would like a career where you have the opportunity to be a leader. You like to influence others and be in charge.

PHYSICAL CHALLENGE: you would like a career where there is a strong physical component to what you do each day.

PRACTICAL: you would like a career where what you do each day is very practical and at the end of the day you can actually see something concrete that you have made, developed or designed.

PRECISE: you would like a career where your work depends on attention to detail.

PRESTIGE: you would like a career where you feel the job is looked upon by others as being prestigious giving you more status in the eyes of yourself and others.

PROBLEM SOLVING: you would like a career where each day there are problems and challenges to solve or resolve.

PUBLIC CONTACT: you would like a career that offers you the opportunity to meet new people each day such as customers and/or clients.

RECOGNITION: you would like a career where you receive recognition and/or respect from others, whether it is from strangers, or from the people you work with.

SERVICE: you would like a career where you assist other people in getting what they want and/or need.

SPIRITUALITY: you would like a career where you work each day with people who have the same spiritual beliefs as you or where you have the opportunity to share your spiritual beliefs with others.

STRUCTURE: you would like a career where there is a set structure and predictability to what you do each day. You tend not to like change.

TEAMWORK: you would like a career where you are often working as part of a team with other people. You like to share ideas with others and work together on projects or assignments.

VARIETY: you would like a career where there is constant variety in what you do each day. You look forward to doing something different each day.

WORK-LIFE BALANCE: you would like a career that provides an opportunity to balance your time with family, hobbies, or other interests with the time necessary to work in your job.

"Know thyself."
Plato

WORLD BETTERMENT: you would like a career where you have the opportunity to make this world a better place to live.

OTHER: perhaps there is a value that is important to you that has not been listed above. If so, write this value or these values below.

_____

> **"It's not hard to make decisions when you know your values."**
> Roy Disney

While it important to consider your values as you plan your future, it is also important to realize that some of your values may change as you get older (as can your interests as well). For example, right now you might value a career where you can do a lot of traveling, but some day when you have children you might not want to travel as much. Similarly right now you might want a career that is a lot of fun even if you are not making very much money, but this value can change once you purchase a car and/or a house, or begin to have other expenses that require you to make more money.

The values that are most important to you are not necessarily the ones that are most important to others. This, along with your own unique interests and abilities, is why you should make your own decisions for your future rather than following what your friends are doing. Choose your own career path, otherwise someone else might choose the wrong one for you. Yes, it is important to get feedback from your family, teachers and friends, but ultimately it is a choice that you will have to make for yourself.

IDENTIFYING YOUR CORE VALUES

On the chart below (BOX #8), identify your top five values from pages 47 - 50 (including any that you wrote yourself on the page 50). It might be helpful for you to read all the values on these pages once again to familiarize yourself with what each of them means. In fact, most people will have to re-read these lists several times in order to identify their top five values. In identifying your top five values, you do not have to place them in priority order - simply write them in any order on the chart below. Remember, you are selecting the values that are most important to you, not the ones you think others want you to list.

advancement

challenge

competitive

creative expression

entrepreneurial

follower

help others

high earnings

independence

knowledge

leadership

physical challenge

practical

precise

prestige

problem solving

public contact

recognition

service

spirituality

structure

teamwork

variety

work-life balance

world betterment

other

THE FIVE VALUES THAT ARE MOST IMPORTANT TO ME

1. . . . .

2. . . . .

3. . . . .

4. . . . .

5. . . . .

BOX 8

ANOTHER LOOK AT MY FUTURE PLANS

INSTRUCTIONS: In BOX #9 below, list the five careers from BOXES 1, 2 + 3 on page 26 and any other occupations from BOX #4 at the bottom of page 31 that you are most interested in.

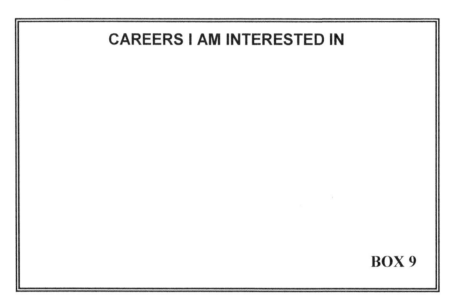

CAREERS I AM INTERESTED IN

BOX 9

INSTRUCTIONS: The careers that you listed above (in BOX #9) were chosen by you based on your interests. On page 51 you identified your top five values. Circle any (or even all) careers in BOX #9 above that have the strongest relationship to your top five values.

In other words, circle any careers in BOX 9 above that would best fulfill or satisfy your values. For instance, if you valued "high earnings", which of the above careers would bring you high earnings? If you valued "challenge", which of the above careers would bring challenges your way?

If you are having any difficulties completing this, ask your teacher/counselor/parents for help.

MY TOP 3 CAREER CHOICES

INSTRUCTIONS: On page 52, you identified a list of your top careers (based on your interests). Next, you circled any occupations in this list that also fulfilled your values. The careers that you circled would appear to be the ones that best match your interests and values.

In BOX 10 below, list the top 3 careers that would seem to best match your interests and values (and these will come from BOX #9 on page 52)

MY TOP 3 CAREER CHOICES
(based on interests and values)

BOX 10

The next chapter will provide a summary of what you have learned so far in this book. It should help you to further clarify possible choices for your future although as it has been previously stated it is okay if you don't know the exact career you want to pursue. As has also been mentioned before in this book, if you are uncertain of your future occupation, you might find it helpful to focus on choosing the best educational/training plan after high school that is based on your strengths (your interests, abilities and values) and then choosing your actual career at some later time. The final two chapters can help you to better set goals for your future based on what you have learned so far in this book.

**Success and happiness
will follow you
when your future plans
are an extension
of who you are.**

SETTING A PLAN FOR YOUR FUTURE

This chapter can help you to establish a plan for your future after high school. As has been stated throughout this book, your best plan will build on your strengths. Some readers may have a clear vision of a future career while others may still be unclear. Regardless, it is important for you to realize that many students successfully plan their future after high school without knowing the exact occupation they want to someday pursue.

As also noted in this chapter, the best way to plan for your future is often to focus right now on being successful in high school. If you establish strong work habits and develop a positive attitude the future will generally be more successful for you even if you are unclear of what you want to someday do in terms of a career or even your education/training after high school.

> **The best way to plan for your future is often to focus right now on being successful in high school.**

> **"The indispensable first step to getting the things you want out of life is this: decide what you want."**
> Ben Stein (actor and author)

> **"You have to believe in yourself when no one else does. That's what makes a winner."**
> Venus Williams
> (Olympic gold medalist and tennis champion)

YOUR SUMMARY

INSTRUCTIONS: In BOX #11 write your top three interests from the bottom of page 25. In BOX #12 write your top three abilities from BOX #5 on page 37. In BOX #13 write your top three values from BOX #8 on page 51.

This provides a summary of the strengths that you have identified for yourself in this book.

MY TOP 3 INTERESTS

1.

2.

3.

(from page 25)　　**BOX 11**

MY TOP 3 ABILITIES

1.

2.

3.

(from page 37)　　**BOX 12**

MY TOP 3 VALUES

1.

2.

3.

(from page 51)　　**BOX 13**

INSTRUCTIONS: In BOX #14 write the three careers that you are most interested in. These careers can come from BOX #7 on page 39 and BOX #10 on page 53.

MY TOP THREE CAREER POSSIBILITIES

1.　　　　　　　　　　2.

(from pages 39 + 53)　　3.

BOX 14

A FUTURE PLAN FOR YOU

As you complete the next few pages, it is strongly recommended that you work with a teacher/counselor and/or your parents to give you feedback on the appropriateness of your plans.

If you are planning to enter the workforce directly from high school, then hopefully you have been able to identify the job/career that you would like to pursue (in BOX #14 on page 56). Next, you should complete pages 58 + 59.

If you are planning on furthering your education/training after high school by attending a college/university or some other educational or career training institution then you should complete page 58 + 60.

Whatever your plans for after high school, one immediate goal should be to graduate from high school. A high school diploma is an important achievement which is often a basic requirement for further education/training and is often a basic requirement for many entry-level jobs. Even if you are uncertain of your future plans you can help to create a better future by focusing on being the best student you can be right now in high school. Page 58 provides an opportunity to summarize the courses you have already completed in high school and then identify the courses (and any other requirements) that you will need to complete to graduate from high school.

For some students, focusing on doing well in high school (which includes strong attendance and working hard in a positive manner to learn as much as possible) may be your best immediate plan to lay the foundation for a successful future, even if you are unsure of your future plans.

The best way to get what you want is to have a clear picture of what it is that you want.

MY HIGH SCHOOL GRADUATION REQUIREMENTS

1. The number of subjects (credits) I need to complete to achieve my high school graduation diploma is . . .

2. The following are the mandatory courses (and any other requirements) I must complete in order to graduate from high school . . .

3. At the current time I have completed . . . . . .high school courses (credits).

4. The following are the mandatory courses (and any other requirements) I still need to complete in order to earn my high school diploma . . .

5. Some other high school courses I still need take to better prepare me for my plans after I graduate from high school are . . .

A PLAN FOR ENTERING THE WORKFORCE

1. An occupation I would like to enter after I complete high school is (see page 56 for help) . . .

2. I believe I would be successful in this occupation because . . .

3. Some companies or businesses that offer this occupation are . . .

4. Two teachers (or coaches, or former employers) I could use as references when I apply for this occupation are . . .

5. After I graduate from high school, if there are no available openings in this occupation, some other jobs I could apply for are . . .

6. Ten years from now, the occupation that I expect to be doing is . . .

A PLAN FOR MY FUTURE EDUCATION/TRAINING

If you already have a clear picture of a future job/career (if you don't have a clear picture of a future occupation, then go to page 61), then you can research more about this career (perhaps you already did this on page 40). By understanding the program you will need to enter in college/university or some other educational/training institution to prepare for this career, you can then look at the high school prerequisites and any other requirements) you will need. The following questions can help you better understand what you need to do in high school to prepare for this career.

1. The occupation that I would like to pursue is . . .

2. I believe I would be successful in this job because . . .

3. A program I could complete after high school to obtain the qualifications for this career is . . .

4. The high school course prerequisites (and any other requirements) I will need to be accepted into this program) are . . .

A PLAN FOR MY FUTURE EDUCATION/TRAINING

If you do not have a clear picture in your mind of a future career, then you can plan your future after high school by identifying your strengths (look at page 56 for help) and then choosing an educational or training program that best matches your strengths. A teacher, career advisor, or counselor can help you with this (and don't forget to include your parents in this process as well).

1. A program (at a college/university or some other training/educational institution) that best matches my strengths is . . .

2. I think this program would be a good choice for me because . . .

3. The high school course prerequisites (and any other requirements) I will need to be accepted into this program) are . . .

4. Some other possible educational/training programs that also match my strengths are . . .

If you knew that you could achieve your dreams, what would you do with your life?

ACHIEVING YOUR GOALS

This final chapter can help you to take what you have learned about yourself so far and begin to establish a plan for your future after high school. To complete this chapter, you will have to spend a little time doing some research. Some high school students resist spending time on planning their future and some of these same students pay a big price down the road when they discover they have chosen the wrong path for their future. Careful planning is an important step towards your future success.

Learning how to set and achieve goals is an important part of being successful. In this chapter you will find some tips on setting goals. You will also find some quotes related to achieving success. As you read these thoughts, it would be useful for you to select one or two tips (or quotes) and write these on a small piece of paper that you carry with you. As you complete pages 65 - 69, you could use pictures instead of words if you want. Success often comes from having a very clear picture of what it is that you want to achieve and then keeping this picture in your mind at all times. It has been said that we become what we think about. Keep your thoughts positive and focused on the goals you want to achieve.

"To tend unfailingly, unflinchingly, towards a goal is the secret of success."
Anna Pavlova

The achievement of any major goal is often the result of establishing a plan of small sequential steps. By working on each step, you can eventually accomplish major goals. Most important of all as you set goals for your future is to remember that any dream you have will always just remain a dream unless you take action.

TIPS ON ACHIEVING YOUR GOALS

1. Always write your goals down.
A goal not written down is not a goal.

2. Spend the greatest amount of your time each day on the things that
will have the greatest impact on achieving your goals.

3. List all the ways both you and others will benefit
when you achieve your goals.

4. Keep a clear vision in your mind that shows you
having already successfully completed your goals.

5. Goals are best achieved when you break them into small,
sequential steps that have appropriate and definite timelines.

6. When you encounter an obstacle,
look for a new path that leads to your desired goal.

7. You can create your own good luck through hard work,
dedication to your goals, and believing you will be successful.

8. The biggest rewards in life are often when you move outside
your own comfort zone. Overcoming your fears
and taking risks often lead to the greatest successes.
Setting goals that will require a great deal of perseverance
often results in greater satisfaction
than quickly accomplishing easier goals.

9. The best way to kill an opportunity is to avoid taking it.
As you focus on your goals, always keep an open mind
for flexible ways of achieving them.

10. After writing down a goal, never leave it without
first taking some positive action towards completing it.

A ONE YEAR PLAN FOR ME

1. A major goal for me once I have graduated from high school is

2. In order for me to achieve this goal, three things I will have to accomplish during this year are

    i)

    ii)

    iii)

3. A date for completing #2 - (i) is

4. A date for completing #2 - (ii) is

5. A date for completing #2 - (iii) is

6. I will know that I have been successful completing #2 - (i) if

7. I will know that I have been successful completing #2 - (ii) if

8. I will know that I have been successful completing #2 - (iii) if

A THREE YEAR PLAN FOR ME

1. A major future goal for me is

2. In order for me to achieve this goal, two things I will have to accomplish for each of the next three years are

YEAR ONE

i)

ii)

YEAR TWO

i)

ii)

YEAR THREE

i)

ii)

3. Dates for completing each the things I need to accomplish according to my answer in question #2 are

    <u>YEAR ONE</u>
    i)
    ii)

    <u>YEAR TWO</u>
    i)
    ii)

    <u>YEAR THREE</u>
    i)
    ii)

4. At the end of the first year I will know I am achieving my goals if

5. At the end of the second year I will know I am achieving my goals if

6. At the end of the third year I will know I am achieving my goals if

A FIVE YEAR PLAN FOR ME

1. A primary occupational goal for me is

2. Ten things I will have to do over the next five years to achieve this goal are

   i)

   ii)

   iii)

   iv)

   v)

   vi)

   vii)

   viii)

   ix)

   x)

3. Place each of the 10 things you identified in #2 on the following timeline giving a specific date as to when you expect to have each thing completed

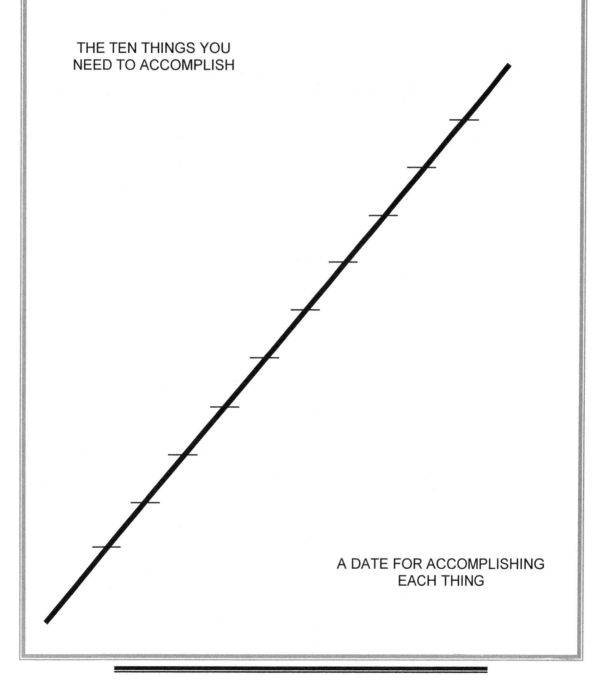

THE TEN THINGS YOU
NEED TO ACCOMPLISH

A DATE FOR ACCOMPLISHING
EACH THING

QUOTES RELATED TO SUCCESS

"Success is not the key to happiness. Happiness is the key to success.
If you love what you are doing, you will be successful."
Albert Schweitzer

"There are no gains without the pains."
Benjamin Franklin

"I know the price of success:
determination, hard work, and a devotion to the things you want to see happen."
F. L . Wright

"Sooner or later, those who win are those that think that they can."
R. Bach

"Success consists of going from failure to failure without loss of enthusiasm."
Winston Churchill

"The greatest barrier to success is the fear of failure."
Sven Goran Erikson

"Success means having the courage, the determination,
and the will to become the person you believe you were meant to be."
G. Sheehan

"Motivation will almost always beat mere talent."
N. R. Augustine

"Nothing will ever be attempted if all possible objections must first be overcome."
S. Johnson

"Many of life's failures are people who did not realize
how close they were to success when they gave up."
Thomas Edison

"Obstacles are those frightful things you see
when you take your eyes off your goal."
Henry Ford

"Action is the foundational key to success."
Pablo Picasso

SOME FINAL THOUGHTS TO HELP YOU ACHIEVE YOUR DREAMS

There have been three underlying themes throughout this book to help you identify and then be successful in achieving your dreams. These three themes are:

1) You Are Responsible For Your Future

2) Build Your Future On Your Strengths

3) Visualize Yourself Being Successful

1) You Are Responsible For Your Future

If you don't have a plan for your future, then someone else is going to make one for you whether it is best for you or not. Some people go through their lives always blaming others for their lack of success. Successful people go through their lives taking responsibility for whatever comes their way. If you find that you are not achieving the success that you would like, then you may need to do things a different way. Change your habits and you can change your outcomes. Successful people develop habits that contribute to being successful. To learn these habits, find someone who is successful and copy what they do.

You may not always be able to change what is happening around you, but you can change yourself. The quality of your life is your choice. This means throwing away any excuses for not being successful. Whenever things don't turn out as you planned, ask yourself, "How can I do it differently next time to get the results that I want?"

> **"Ninety-nine percent of all failures come from people who have a habit of making excuses."**
> G. W. Carver

> **"Decide upon your major definite purpose in life and then organize all your activities around it."**
> Brian Tracey

2) Build Your Future On Your Strengths

We all have an inner guidance system. When your goals are in harmony with your interests, abilities and values you will find the greatest joy and success in all that you do. When you focus your time and energy doing the things you really love and are good at, you will eventually receive huge rewards.

Every day think about what it is that you do really well. Constantly build on your strengths. When your future goals are based on your loves, you will achieve your greatest results. To achieve your goals, you may have to say "NO" when others try to steer you in another direction. The difference between success and failure for most people is simply a matter of focus. Take a little time throughout each day to ensure you are focusing on achieving YOUR goals.

3) Visualize Yourself Being Successful

Whatever you think about the most, you will tend to become. Start each day by writing down your goals. Always keep a clear picture of your dreams in your mind. When you do this, your subconscious will help you work towards accomplishing these dreams. Constantly visualize yourself as being successful in achieving your dreams. Whenever you find yourself thinking about failure, STOP and change your thinking.

Whatever you believe is true will lead you towards that reality. Focus on where you want to go, not your fears. Create goals that you get excited about and remember the first step in any success begins when you take ACTION!

"To laugh often
and much;
To win the respect
of intelligent people
and the affection
of children;
To earn the
appreciation
of honest critics and
endure the betrayal
of false friends;
To appreciate beauty,
to find the best
in others;
To leave the world
a bit better,
whether by a
healthy child,
a garden patch
or a redeeming
social condition;
To know even one life
has breathed easier
because you
have lived;
This is to have
succeeded."
Bessie Stanley

NOTES

COLLEGE SUCCESS

Tips From A College Professor

Brian Harris, B.A., M.Ed.

THE
STUDENT
SUCCESS
HANDBOOK

125 Ready-To-Use Activities
Includes activity handouts and a 68 page student workbook

Brian Harris, B.A. M.Ed.

SELF-ESTEEM

150 Ready-to-use Activities to Enhance the Self-Esteem of Children
and Teenagers to Increase Student Success and Improve Behavior

Book 1

Brian Harris, B.A. M.Ed.

MY FUTURE

**150 Ready-to-use Career/Educational Planning
Activities for High School Students**

Brian Harris, B.A. M.Ed.

About the Author

Brian Harris is an award-winning teacher/counselor and best-selling author. He has extensive experience in working with children of all ages in elementary schools, high schools, colleges and universities. He has also achieved the designation of International Professional Speaker. He has extensive experience in the field of educational/career planning as well as self-esteem.

Brian lives in Burlington, Canada, with his wife and two teenage daughters. In addition to writing, Brian is a part-time lecturer in counseling at Queen's University. He is also an accomplished artist (www.bcharris.com).

Brian enjoys family trips and is an avid canoeist and scuba diver.

Additional information about Brian can be found at
www.cgscommunications.com

Made in the USA
Columbia, SC
08 November 2020